W9-APB-022

Rapture

ALSO BY SUSAN MITCHELL

The Water Inside the Water

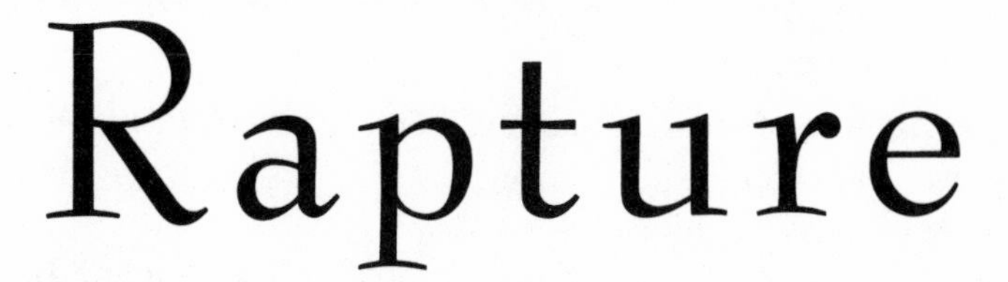

poems by

Susan Mitchell

HarperPerennial
A Division of HarperCollins*Publishers*

It is a pleasure to thank The National Endowment for the Arts, The Illinois Arts Council, The Vermont Arts Council, and The Florida Division of Cultural Affairs for grants of support that made this writing possible.

Grateful acknowledgment is made to the following publications in which some of these poems have appeared:

The American Poetry Review: "Rainbow," "Self-Portrait with Two Faces"

The Atlantic: "Bus Trip"

Crazyhorse: "A Story," "Cities"

Ironwood: "Leaves That Grow Inward," "Smoke," "The Hotel by the Sea"

The Nation: "Fragment of a Woman from Kos"

The New Yorker: "Women in Profile: Bas-Relief, Left Section Missing"

Ploughshares: "Havana Birth," "Aviary," "Night Music," "The Child Bride" under the title "Children's Ward: New York Hospital"

Provincetown Arts: "Sky of Clouds"

The Quarterly: "Feeding the Ducks at the Howard Johnson Motel"

Tikkun: "The Return of Jonah by Way of Swanawic as Recorded by a West Saxon Scribe, 871 A.D."

"Havana Birth" was also collected in *Best American Poetry 1990.*

"A Story" was also collected in *New American Poets of the Eighties.*

"Sky of Clouds" was also collected in *Best American Poetry 1991.*

"Leaves That Grow Inward" was also collected in *The Pushcart Prize XIII.*

HarperCollins books may be purchased for educational, business, or sales promotional use. For information, please call or write: Special Markets Department, HarperCollins Publishers, Inc., 10 East 53rd Street, New York, NY 10022. Telephone: (212) 207-7528; Fax: (212) 207-7222.

FIRST EDITION

Designed by Cassandra Pappas

LIBRARY OF CONGRESS CATALOGING-IN-PUBLICATION DATA

Mitchell, Susan, 1944–
Rapture / Susan Mitchell.
p. cm.
ISBN 0-06-055320-0 / ISBN 0-06-096906-7 (pbk.)
I. Title.
PS3563.I824R36 1992 91-50517
811'.54—dc20

92 93 94 95 96 PS/HC 10 9 8 7 6 5 4 3 2 1
92 93 94 95 96 PS/HC 10 9 8 7 6 5 4 3 2 1 (pbk.)

Contents

Three

One

Havana Birth

Off Havana, the ocean is green this morning
of my birth. The conchers clean their knives on leather
straps and watch the sky while three couples
who have been dancing on the deck of a ship
in the harbor, the old harbor of the fifties, kiss
each other's cheeks and call it a night.

On a green sofa five dresses wait
to be fitted. The seamstress kneeling at Mother's feet
has no idea I am about to be born. Mother
pats her stomach which is flat
as the lace mats on the dressmaker's table. She thinks
I'm playing in my room. But as usual, she's wrong.

I'm about to be born in a park in Havana. Oh,
this is important, everything in the dressmaker's house
is furred like a cat. And Havana leans right up
against the windows. In the park, the air
is chocolate, the sweet breath of a man
smoking an expensive cigar. The grass

is drinkable, dazzling, white. In a moment
I'll get up from a bench, lured
by a flock of pigeons, lazily sipping
the same syrupy music through a straw.
Mother is so ignorant, she thinks
I'm rolled like a ball of yarn under the bed. What

does she know of how I got trapped in my life?
She thinks it's all behind her, the bloody
sheets, the mirror in the ceiling
where I opened such a sudden furious blue, her eyes
bruised shut like mine. The pigeon's eyes
are orange, unblinking, a doll's. Mother always said

I wanted to touch everything because
I was a child. But I was younger than that.
I was so young I thought whatever I
wanted, the world wanted too. Workers
in the fields wanted the glint of sun on their machetes.
Sugarcane came naturally sweet, you

had only to lick the earth where it grew.
The music I heard each night outside
my window lived in the mouth of a bird. I was so young
I thought it was easy as walking
into the ocean which always had room
for my body. So when I held out my hands

I expected the pigeon to float between them
like a blossom, dusting my fingers with the manna
of its wings. But the world is wily, and doesn't want
to be held for long, which is why
as my hands reached out, workers lay down
their machetes and left the fields, which is why

a prostitute in a little *calle* of Havana dreamed
the world was a peach and flicked
open a knife. And Mother, startled, shook
out a dress with big peonies splashed like dirt
across the front, as if she had fallen
chasing after me in the rain. But what could I do?

I was about to be born, I was about to have
my hair combed into the new music
everyone was singing. The dressmaker sang it, her mouth
filled with pins. The butcher sang it and wiped
blood on his apron. Mother sang it and thought her body
was leaving her body. And when I tried

I was so young the music beat right
through me, which is how the pigeon got away.
The song the world sings day after day
isn't made of feathers, and the song a bird pours
itself into is tough as a branch
growing with the singer and the singer's delight.

The Hotel by the Sea

In the hotel by the sea a man is playing the piano.
The piano wants to be played
like a pinball machine, it wants the man to lean his weight
against the music until the sound tilts. But the man
wanders inside the piano like someone looking
for an elevator in a drafty building
or like a drunk who can't find
his way in a song he keeps repeating.

The piano wants to play leaky faucets and water running
all night in the toilets of a train station.
It wants to play obscenities
and the delicate moths that scratch their bellies
on the ballroom screens.
The piano wants to scratch. It wants to spit
on the pavement. It wants to look into stores where women
try on clothes and open their thighs to the mirrors.

The piano wants to be a fat woman. It wants to play
baggy and flab and carry tuna sandwiches to work
in brown paper. It wants to dress up in sequins and eat
fried fish. It wants to suck its fingers and flick
ashes into the ocean. And it wants to squeeze
into a single note,
a silvery tube, and hold its breath.
The piano tells the man to forget everything

he ever learned and play the music boys pass in secret
from desk to desk at school, the blue saliva
of their kisses. The man feels left out of
this music and thinks of going for cigarettes.
The piano wants to drink up
the butts littering the ballroom.
It wants to sit down on the dance floor
and sob with joy, it wants to rub

all memory of celebration from the man's fingers.
The piano wants to blow its nose
in the music and play the silence of the room and the rain
falling outside. It wants to play the pores
in the man's face and his chapped hands.
The piano wants the man to dance
in his sports shirt and floppy pants.
It wants him to ride up and down

the hotel elevators and follow women back
to their rooms. It wants him to pull roses from their hair
and mice and light up like an arcade.
The piano is sick and tired
of this man's hands which sit down
on their grief, as on a jetty, and count the stars.
The piano doesn't care about hard times.
It wants to stay up all night

and tell unrepeatable stories to the ocean.
It wants a sound to come
from this man's mouth, even though his teeth
are picked clean.
The man won't know the sound
when he makes it. He'll think a woman is kissing Kleenex.
He'll think it's 4 A.M. and he can't buy
a pack of anything anywhere.

The Child Bride

This time, Death is rising, waving its big bird
wing, anthracite plume, smoke and smudge of a twilit sky
E. A. Poe would have delighted in. Along the river
lights spread, bridges sway into brilliance, it's all
so sudden, like coming out of anesthesia, gates
opening, ascent and arrival, the elevator lifting
suavely into consciousness. But no,

I am leaving the hospital, thinking of the woman Poe
almost married, and if he had, there wouldn't be that story
of the child bride, eight years old when Edgar
fell in love with her, same age as Dante's Beatrice.
Paradise is what Dante did with loss. But try
to imagine what it would be like to break
bad news to Poe, stare him straight in the eyes

and say, Listen, it's over, *fini*, ended, as far
as you're concerned, she's dead, you
understand, dead. I'd rather take out the hospital garbage,
or breathe ether, handkerchief pressed
to my face, swilling big gulps
of forgetfulness, swinging me darker
with the gulls that swim among skyscrapers, slashes of black—

Ah, sleep. Ah, the long swoon. In the hospital
is a corridor amuck with children, cages,
carriages, bed trays, wheelchairs in long lines
as in an airport. Children, children everywhere.
So much in life is a mystery to me,
pain is a mystery and pleasure, water is and Poe
who said *I could not bring my passions from a common*
  spring.

I am a mystery to myself, especially now
as I leave the hospital in memory, this phantom who hails
a cab to a bar on Third, and first thing,
examines her face in the Ladies' mirror, pencils
her lips blood red. In October the river
wind almost overpowers the fumes of buses, holds me
down in the deep pungencies of my suede jacket—

marigold, Cabochard, perfume no longer
obtainable on this earth. The children always died
in another language, though, I might add, don't we all,
misunderstood to the very end. Mainly, the language they
died in was Spanish. But sometimes they died in *transistor*.
Sometimes in *window,* a transparency that looks out on
the world, leading the tongue to new adventures

like a good lover. With leukemia, a strange thing can
happen even as the doctors are paged and a visitor leafs
  through
magazines. The patient, if male, feels a sudden tumescence
that will not go down, and at first, this seems the promise
of recovery, a fountain of youth, this rigor
mortis of the nerves, catalepsy of blood ending in
stalagmite, that true red marble called *rosso*

antico, oxides of iron, ferruginous, pegged to
falsetto, the veins of the penis standing out
in bas-relief, shadow and duct, reddish mottled stone. This can
happen to a boy, too, and perhaps that's what is meant
by the old cliché, The dying see their lives
flash before them—the doctors running, nurses
crowding the room, the parents told to step outside—

because in that instant the boy is a man, and in hours
the boy-man is taken up to surgery
where something is cut, a nerve or a vein, which proves
what a terrible thing desire is, how wanting
so strongly cannot be borne for long, it is
necessary to rub the body against stone,
roughen the penis with the tough

calluses of the hands until nothing
is left. Of course, it is possible to outlive
desire and be an Abelard untouched by tears, by the body
secreting itself in salts of grief and love, never
running barefoot through the dirty city
snow to where someone disappears into a taxi, into the speed
and thrust of exit so powerful, it's almost

possible to hear its crash and cymbals. In the Middle Ages
there were manuals, *ars moriendi,* that taught
the novice how to die well, step
by step of the deep declivity. You, even I,
could learn to visualize a sick man in bed, the skeletal
Death approaching with club raised, ready
to strike. Let me be

your example and mirror is the Image's request, the sick
man inviting the visitor to slip under the covers
of his skin, be his terror, be
the rubber retainer inside his mouth, feel
teeth biting down on, bear its imprint,
as he does, with patience. But desire does not die
easy. Inside the folds of Egyptian mummies,

crushed deep into inner sanctums of linen,
the linen calcified, welded with flesh, archaeologists
find beetles so desperate for food they ate
through the body's silks and wrappings. Desire goes on,
ravenous, consumed and consuming as the simple
thing a child was doing before the first twinge
of illness, a thing so ravishing now

the child can't get enough, it keeps staring
out a window where I see only people waiting
for a bus, keeps staring at a wall
where I see only knobs and wheels
and a stain that looks like a fist or small animal
clenched into a ball. But something else
must be there or why would the child

keep staring, playing the wall over and over
like the bars of a favorite song. Poe's child
bride was singing when she had her first hemorrhage,
as if music and blood flow from the same vein and the heart
can pump only so much. The song split, traveling
in two directions, and one was a foreign
country always out of reach, a bird singing

in a forest she could not enter, though Poe
described it for her, a place where *strange brilliant*
flowers, star-shaped, burst out upon the trees
where no flowers had been known before. The children's ward
extends for miles, there are so many
rooms, who could enter them all, who could
map the hidden corridors, the series of basements below

the first floor where white arrows and yellow arrows guide
the visitor to doors that open onto other doors.
It runs so far in, like pain itself,
chamber opening into chamber, the music intensifying,
changing key, modulating into, radiating—
the entire history of human suffering force fed,
dripped into the arm drop by drop, the lime

grottoes building slowly, the weird formations
opening onto banquet halls hung
with icicles and stony curtains, the grottoes pulsating
as they grow, each note dripped
lifts me by the hair until I forget
the name of my own country, forget
which language is which.

Leaves That Grow Inward

So you see, it was my favorite time
for waking, toward evening, when the lights came on
all together like candles on a child's cake.
I would yawn, as if just leaving a movie.
The better part of the day was over, no longer
a chance of doing anything worthwhile.
The relief of it. This was the hour
I took my bath as a child,
not always alone, sometimes with a friend, Clara,
whose left arm ended abruptly at the elbow,
as if she had managed to draw up
inside her the hand, its fingers, even
a small object the fingers had been holding
at the time this miracle occurred. If
I had known Hölderlin's poem about the leaves
that grow inward, I would have recited it
to her, *hängen einwärts die Blätter,*
as she splashed water in my face
with that budding stump of hers. Once
at this hour my mother plucked a snail
from watercress, a black glistening that sweated
across my palm. Clara held it too
with her eyes, the way I held her
in the school playground until all at once
I heard the train, still far away, that brought
my father from his office, its wind
blowing on the lights of our street.

Sometimes all my childhood burns like a fever,
even my mother's hand on my forehead
as she urges me to practice
the piano, as she tells me to drink the music
like blood, holding my cramped

fingers under running water
until somewhere in the street a child lets out
a long necklace of sounds, a crying
that gradually loosens itself
from whatever flesh has held it. It
is not easy, it is like pulling hairs
from the tenderest parts
of the body. . . . Only, to tell the truth, there
never was a Clara, a point I might confess
to a psychiatrist. Instead
I confess it to myself, waiting
for illumination, eyes closed,
but still seeing as if through leaves, through the sap
of my cells. . . . At school, there was
a girl like her, but her arm
terrified me. I withdrew
from it. Which is quite another
thing, isn't it? Though in the safety of my bath
she sometimes entered my life as a possibility
of future loss. So, you see,
I am not the person you thought I was,
the one you had grown comfortable with, maybe
even liked a little.
Liking,
our first grade teacher used to say, begins
with proximity, as before—waking
into a day already over, I heard
the high rise in which I live talking
to itself, moaning like the sea
or like someone stumbling in and out
of sleep. The building was neither happy nor sad,
but continuous, one of those
unending songs a child sings to itself.

The grief of my neighbors, the grief of all
the neighbors I have ever had is
another story, the secret
lint a child digs from its navel
while its fingers age in the bath. What
would it have been like to be the one who played
with Clara, whooping down on the neighborhood
bakery, mouth stuffed with strudel, not caring
if my tongue scorched and blistered? What would it
have been like to hold
the sticks of dog shit, the purified chalk
they scrawled their names with? At the edges
of memory, Clara glimmers, beckoning
as if into a forest. Striped with desires
more bruising than prison bars, she leans out of
herself, toward a flashing on the pavement,
toward snow greened with dog piss.

Well, life
is better now, and sometimes I consume
four movies in a day, surprised, as I drift
to the street, it's dark outside too, surprised
to see people waiting to see what I have just seen.
This is the hour when two men
kiss in the elevator, a long kiss,
which stops only as an old woman gets on,
then they hold hands. Half asleep,
I hear them kissing and the sky
darkening, washing out to the Hudson
where the freighters kneel in the sailors' shadows
and kids tripping on acid come
to watch the men knotting
and unknotting in their ecstasies.

Even from here I follow their brief spurts
of pleasure, the tides of clouds, until I feel far
as someone drifting in a boat
or waving from a train a paper
hat, while the dark snails of my flesh slide
toward some heaven of their own.

Smoke

At night the child takes down
the helmet and puts it on, the bullet hole
facing front. It does this in secret,
standing on the bed

to make itself bigger,
a dark figure confronting the mirror. God knows
who the helmet belonged to, the father
brought it back from a war

along with the gun which the child
plays with now that the firing pin's removed.
The mother hates the helmet with its leather
chin strap and hides it

in the closet. The child
wants to drink the shadows at the bottom
where a man lived, where he put his hair and brains
and kept his cigarettes.

No one likes the child
to point the gun at them. The child asks,
Did you kill anyone? pointing
the gun at the father,

and frankly, is disappointed
by the answer. The mirror does not disappoint
the child. At night it fills with shadows and barbed
wire and the dead soldier

who comes to talk in German,
which the child does not understand, saying
only *Ja, ja.* The soldier is careful
to stand on his side

of the mirror. Sometimes
the child steals a cigarette from the mother's
bag, but the soldier prefers his own. So,
the child lights up for itself,

taking a long drag
as it lies back in bed, the lighted end
all that's visible in the dark.
It is strange to think

when the child grows up
this is how she will look after making
love, holding the smoke in her mouth
as if it were precious.

The Kiss

He said I want to kiss you in a way
no one has ever kissed you before, a kiss
so special you will never forget and no one will ever

we had moved into a room away
from the others where coats were piled
on a bed, and in the almost dark the kiss began
to assume baroque proportions, expanding
and contracting like a headache   pushing winglike

from my feet. In adolescent fantasies I used to
think of myself in the third
person so that when I kissed for the first
time in a film of my own making a voice
kept saying Now he is kissing her, now she is
unbuttoning her blouse, now his hand

the voice just ahead of the picture or the sex
lagging always behind as in a badly
dubbed film   the voice

trying clumsily to undress them, hiding
behind a screen or hovering above the bed dovelike
a Holy Spirit of invention presiding over each
nipple, enticing erect the body's
erectile tissue, inflaming their eyes

to see in the dark hiddenness
of wordless doing, to watch, to keep watching
to the edge of, the verging precipice beyond which
language, thought's emissary huffing
and puffing, or beyond which language's undercover
agent and spy, thought.   Now thinking back to

that time, I am always just behind myself
like a shadow, I am muteness
about to blossom   into mystic vision   or with some word

stick a pin into, fasten like a butterfly
on black velvet, though it seems forever since I
kissed the back of my hand, pretending
my hand was my mouth, my mouth
the man's, in order to know what a kiss was, teeth
gently pulling at the skin on top
near the knuckles, the way a cat lifts
its kitten by the nape of the neck, dragging it
to a dark place under a house, or

licking the inside of my hand up the heart
line, down the life line   I don't

remember who left the room first, though
when someone told me he was
a famous director, I watched more intently
as he held out a canapé
to his wife.
                    Sometimes in the years
that followed I thought of him, his ornate
description of the kiss, which with time became
more ornate, his tongue glossing

the whorls and bric-a-brac, the Adirondack
antlers on the grotesque banquettes, the kiss
coiling round itself like a snail

a small Gongoresque affair with all its
engines thrumming, that description the most
memorable thing about him whose face, if I ever
really looked at it, I have forgotten,
whose mouth, whose teeth, whose tongue
did not open anything in me
but directly

presented themselves as one takes a pear or apple
into one's hand and walks down the street
not thinking about the apple
or pear, but simply eating.

Wave

I don't mean this as a command, though
if you want to wave to someone
there's no reason why you shouldn't.
I'll go on looking out this window, pretending
you're not here, not doing something
as ridiculous as jerking your hand
up and down. I'm devoted
to an enormous expanse of violet
which is how the Atlantic wants to be today.
Cutting across the violet are gigantic
stripes of green and within
the green stripes
which are swelling, breathing deeply, the sun
encaged like a canary.
If that's too difficult to visualize,
think of a green grape inside
lime Jell-O, the frigid
cafeteria air, the iced celery,
the chartreuse translucency
you are about to take into your mouth.
Its palpitations.
On the horizon is a freighter and maybe
this is what you have been waving at,
a very complicated rig
resembling the skyline of a major city
with smokestacks and fire escapes.
It reminds me of those complex
apparatuses Freud's patients dreamed about—
ingenious metaphors for the urinary tract
or genitals. There is even something red
on the rig like the wattles of a turkey.
But if you are not waving
at the freighter, then maybe

it's that sparkle jumping about
like batons, like rhinestone drumsticks.
My Atlantic is cat's-paw, a purpurate
empurpling into which I yearn
violently to be dipped,
rubbed against the many ink pads
of the ocean. But since the water
is violetted only from this distance, its methyls
dissolving as one gets close enough
to feel the scratch of floating sargasso
my appetite is impossible to gratify.
To come up close on such purples,
such spangles, we'd have to find some cheap
bazaar, a flea market where the heaps
of scarves, the gauzy, flimsy
costumes have been steeped
in Tyre, though once real kings and queens
went everywhere in such frieze and panelwork
with cloaks of night-sky and constellations.
I envy birds of prey, how they don't
waver as they come in close,
how they undress the tassels and pom-poms,
the nosegay heads, the lacework
of the little birds, how
they ankle and beak in furbelows
of blood. But hush. Here it comes, what
I've been waiting for, the smash
and loops of wave on wave,
this crested cobra
towering above. What membrane
keeps that transparency
from dispersing into air the way

Cities

1

Like a branch snapped off from a tree its five
buds slicked down, lacquered hard like a spike
like a tine a rod of buds disconnected
from a magnolia about to bloom—

I went to visit a friend, the hospital
room dark except for the branch
I placed in a vase before leaving,
so she might hear the buds
open, no lid no roof for them, as they persisted
in blooming, though severed,
isolated from the tree, sweating
from the effort of breaking open, the petals damp
as if running uphill, as if this coming
into blossom were a race, this
opening, all five together, an ache in
the side of the tree, the fragile
anther gasped out—

Like a branch that blooms in a vase just as a tree
comes into bloom on the street where

Like a branch that keeps its pact
with a tree, that remembers the moment agreed on

2

In the city where I was born the lights have come on
and even here, two thousand miles away
it feels like a slap
in the face, a gunshot—like that, zap, you're

dead and risen into light salty and fried
blue, then dipped in despair. In the city where I
was born, the lights come on
like a come-on, a chorus of altos and sopranos

surging through millions of filaments. The aria
I'm so at home in, reciting the names
of streets by heart when all at once the bridges
blow back like burning ash

from a thousand cigarettes—I am breathing that
exhalation the city gives off at night,
its lights another city miraculously
held aloft, an ocean where neon

fish tango the expressways. In the city
where I was born, the lights
froth on like a come-on, and if I stood fluttering

high above other roofs and ledges,
it would seem an easy thing
to sacrifice my hands, even the scarf at my throat
to blare out over streets where cartons

are stacked and burning in the center
lane and shopping bags of light ripped and torn
open spill great sheaves of gold into the high winds
of sirens and trucks shifting gear

3

For some things there is no cure.

There are distractions.

There are long gloves of champagne suede with pearl
buttons that take forever to fasten
into delicate loops

and cafés with marble tables where at twilight
one sits drinking Punt e Mes or
Cinzano and watches the faces gleam, candles
behind the steamed restaurant windows.

There are operas and gondolas and metros
where Pound saw petals on a wet, black bough.

At this hour men and women twitter like birds.

Men and women come together in flocks.

When I think of all the conversations I have
drifted out of like smoke, how little
I meant to any of them, how easily
they went on without help from me—

In Paris I went to the cinema every night,
though I understood little
the actors said. I let the images
wash over me: a woman undressing, the black lace
of her hair and the nervous flicks of ash
as a man waited for her in bed.

I entered the movies as if they were houses of worship.

Afterward, walking with the crowds along
Quai d'Orsay I thought of the many locks I had
to open to enter the building where I lived.

In Rome where the prostitutes paint their eyelids
the aged copper of urns and wait
in front of their Cadillacs and Chevys, I thought of
Keats and stood before the house

where he died. In Rome where the prostitutes
remove their heads and stare
as statues stare, with their bodies, I reread
the odes. And in Florence
I thought of Dante and tried to imagine the bridges
to God's kingdom strummed with lights, the distances

played on flute and viola da gamba. In Florence
I turned again to the cantos. But it was
spring, and I let the book drop
like a burning brand, words and blood
hissed out from the branch

Dante broke, the pages plucked
from Hell. And it seemed then that trying to keep
oneself from entering the city of one's birth
must be like refusing to visit a great
love, the body tearing its own knots, the woman's face
or the man's always pressed to the window
of memory, though now

4

of each day when waves of darkness rush
toward shore, flooding houses and cars, and across

the canal, the streetlights send
down golden roots
into the black water, the roots swaying, tangling
into an enormous forest of gold

it seems more like learning to breathe
under water for longer and longer
intervals. Or learning to sing under water as certain

birds do here on this barrier reef at the end
of each day when waves of darkness rush
toward land, flooding houses and cars and across

5

I want something else in my mouth

Bread and butter, coffee and cream, blink and stutter

In the city where I was born
but not so fast—

I want something other
the *cough* in *coffee* and the *cawf* in *cough*
the *dog* in *doggerel* and the *dawg* in *dog,* not *god*
but *gawd.* Forget *gaudy,* forget *gaudeamus igitur.* I want
the gutter in *guttural* and syllables like crates loaded
onto barges rusted, planks swollen, gangrenous, bitter

as iodine and its ignominies, the conglomerates stuffed
into my mouth before my tongue
was pulled out by the roots, I want my crooked teeth,
  language
before orthodontia, the sounds unbarred, the buck

and buckle and overlap, Bunny Mouth, Weasel Face, Crocodile
  Kid

tongue crushed, slummed in, no room to turn around, so
pointed straight out at, the famous legs kicked
forward and back, enfilade, chorus line,
not a heartbeat skipped: spank fire waves strutting
toward shore—sync or sink—tasseled, fringed, foam flung
  behind

and on the esplanades the women softly aglow, the boulevards
transversed with lights, the cars in slow motion and what
was tossed from windows scattering sparks, its hundred
portals open to the sea and

the languages undressed to lamb's wool and perspiration

I be leaving this address
I be seeing you some time, adios, ciao, I be going now, the
  present
tense drawn out like a long kiss, the slow raptures of now

pressed mouth to mouth (we rode the same subways, we
  chewed the same
gum, and remember how it was returning home with someone
else's hair stuck to our coats, the transfers
during rush-hour crushes, the lint from the other

sweaters stuck to our sleeves, their thistle-fuzz, the Day-Glo
  seeds
vendors passed in the dark tunnels, the *gelati,* orange roe

of sea) the lights still on at eight A.M., pale anemic hiss
of fluorescence in the all-night donut shop, columns of
women in floor-length gowns, their lithe arms irriguous,
faces shot through with metallic iridescence
of recently excavated Roman glass

6

Not the clouds at dawn, their fringed edges, the silken
  raspberry folds.
Not the clouds puffed up, frothing over slate stairways,
the columns bituminous, elevators ascending.
Not the promenades flung out white

porticoes where window shoppers in plush furs bristling
with snow brush powder

                                        not the demolishing, the wide blue
vistas through which walls are seen crumbling
the spaces broadening to let in arches and the tall
bays of the basilicas—

The master fashioned a city. He called it Purgatory, he called
it Hell, to replace the woman he lost.
And when the city was lost, he remembered
the woman and closed his eyes

to find his way down the narrow lanes
the *vincula,* the alleys and berms, when over the river
anthracite steeples proffered like hucksters.

But when were similitudes ever enough?
It's the visible
flesh that's craved. Give me one good story to lean my face
into, sleeve of a coat, softly padded shoulder—

There was a story someone entrusted to you,
like Mother's pearls, or postcards from the dead.
You forgot it, had something else to do.

There was a city, *whilom,* made from glue
and paper, a party favor. In its streets you read
a story someone intended only for you.

The story had height and a bright avenue
of bars. At night it burned beside the bed.
You closed your eyes, had something else to do.

There was a story blurted out while you
were drinking, and all the ones who heard
looked down, a story confided in you.

Maybe the dead are the ones you should tell it to.
It's always about them, what they said.
There was a story. It was entrusted to you.
Well, forget it now. The dead have something else to do

blubbering in the gullies of deep space, beyond
the Great Divide, beyond the sticks and boonies—

I have tried saying this in other ways. Toward evening, I have
waited in the outskirts where no bus comes, where no train
and the tracks grown over with purple flowers. I covered
my ears when the jets flew in low
on their way to the airport. I stood on the siding near

the switchback, the sunset spectacular behind the gas
tanks and viaducts, the bridge cables on fire

I stood wide
of the mark and listened to the hyperborean boom of
trucks on the elevated highways, the split and fissure of steel
joints, seams astonishing from underneath where dark pools

of rain never dry, but deepen into bunkers and wadi,
pitchholes,
the punch and gouge where steam shovel and crane—

When I reached the construction site, it was boarded up,
the faces of movie actresses and handsome men
drinking scotch peeled from the faces
of movie actresses and men in red automobiles

A Story

There is a bar I go to when I'm in Chicago
which is like a bar I used to go to when I lived in New York.
There are the same men racing toy cars
at a back table, the money passing so fast
from hand to hand, I never know who's winning, who's losing,
only in the New York bar the racers sport Hawaiian shirts
while in the Chicago bar they wear Confederate caps
with crossed gold rifles pinned to their bands.
Both bars have oversized TVs and bathrooms
you wouldn't want to be caught dead in,
though some have. Once in the New York bar I watched a
  film
on psychic surgery, and I swear to you
the surgeon waved a plump hand—
the hand hovered like a dove over the patient's back,
and where wings grow out of an angel's shoulders
a liquid jetted, a clear water, as if pain
were something you could see into like a window.
Later, walking home with a friend
who was also a little drunk, I practiced psychic surgery
on our apartment building, passing my hands
back and forth over the bricks.
I don't know what I expected to happen,
maybe I hoped a pure roach anguish would burst forth.
But there was only the smell that rises out of New York City
in August, a perennial urine—dog, cat, human—
the familiar stench of the body returning to itself as alien.
Sometimes, before stopping in at the Chicago bar,
I would either sleep or go for a walk,
especially in October when the leaves had turned red.
As they swept past me, I thought of my blood
starting to abandon my body,
taking up residence elsewhere like the birds

gathering in feverish groups on the lawns.
In the Chicago bar there were men who never watched TV
or played the video games, mainly from the Plains tribes they
sat in silence over their whiskey, and looking at them,
I could even hear the IRT as it roared through
the long tunnel between Borough Hall and Wall Street,
the screech of darkness on steel.
And it happened one night that a man,
his hair loose to his shoulders, stood up and pulled
a knife from his boot, and another man
who must have been waiting all his life for this
stood up in silence too, and in seconds
one of them was curled around the knife in his chest
as if it were a mystery he would not reveal to anyone.
Sometimes I think my life is what I keep escaping.
Staring at my hands, I almost expect them to turn
into driftwood, bent and polished by the waves,
my only proof I have just returned from a long journey.
The night Tom Littlebird killed Richard Highwater
with a knife no one knew he carried, not even
during the five years he spent at Stateville,
I thought of men and women who sell their blood for
a drink of sleep in a doorway or for a bus ticket
into a night which is also a long drink to nowhere,
and I thought of the blood I was given
when I was nineteen, one transfusion for each year of my life,
and how I promised myself,
if I lived, I would write a poem in honor of blood.
First for my own blood which,
like the letter that begins the alphabet,
is a long cry AAAAH! of relief.
Praise to my own blood which is simple
and accepts almost anything.

And then for the blood that wrestled
all night with my blood
until my veins cramped and the fingers of one hand went
  rigid.

Praise to the blood that wanted to remain alone,
weeping into its own skin,
so that when it flowed into me, my blood contracted
on the knot in its throat. For you
who raised a rash on my arms
and made my body shiver for days, listen,
whoever you are, this poem is for you.

Bus Trip

All across America children are learning to fly.
On a bus leaving New Hampshire, on a bus
leaving Colorado, I sat next to a child

who had learned how to fly
and she carried her flying clenched
inside both fists. She carried her flying

in a suitcase and in a stuffed dog
made of dirt and the places where she had stood
all night listening to the rain. A child sits

on the roof of a house, she dangles
first one leg, then the other,
as if she were thinking

of how America looks late at night
through the windows of a bus.
From a woman across the aisle, she borrows

a mirror, from a woman in the back
a lipstick. *Keep it,* a voice says.
From a man she takes a cigarette,

which she taps against her thigh.
The man closes his eyes
over her body, such a small body

he could lift it to his mouth
with one hand. In a bathroom she buys a comb
with a quarter borrowed from me

and insists I write down
my name and address so she can return it
from L.A. or from Chicago or from wherever it is

someone she hasn't met yet is waiting for her.
In the dark of the bus she combs her hair.
And what she says to me is a song

that takes only three minutes
to hear, which I accept
like a stick of gum. *Now you tell me*

the songs you like best,
she says.
And I do.

Rainbow

I said to my mother, Look at the rainbow.
We were walking along a street that ran parallel
with the Atlantic, and though the day had been hot
and muggy, because of the storm going on
somewhere to the east, there was a chill.
I had my arm around my mother to keep her warm.
The rainbow was mainly violets and purples
with some pink and green and it stood
out against the sky which was black.
How many miles it spanned
before it sank at either end into the ocean
like the pylons of a bridge or how deep
under the waves I couldn't say.
The colors appeared solid as rock, so
I let myself go with a fantasy—
fish swimming around and under, barnacles
and snails attaching to the lavenders
and grapes, the violets. Now, my mother
is the kind of person—well, if she came on
a rainbow in a poem, she would say
sentimental, she would tell the poet
to take it out. She is a great lover of poetry
and has always disliked sentimentality
in art. One night she called me
from Connecticut and asked if I had
the *Oxford Book of German Verse*
which she had used at college.
The poem she wanted me to read to her
was Goethe's "Das Veilchen" or "The Violet."
She kept correcting my pronunciation
so we went slowly and when she asked
if I knew what this or that phrase

meant, usually I didn't so she was translating
word for word. Because of the slow, tedious way
in which we were reading the poem, I felt
as if we were building it together
solidly in the air between us, the fourteen
hundred miles from Connecticut to Florida.
The poem hung there, it held
in all that space. What amazed me
was how the poem was not at all
sentimental even though the speaker
is a violet pulled up and looked at for a while
because people are attracted to its beauty;
for a while they hold it
in their hands before throwing it away
to die alongside the road. When we finished
reading my mother said this verse
was her favorite, which took me by surprise, I
would never have guessed, never
in a million years, so all at once
something opened up in the space
between us and something else vanished.
I tried to explain this to a friend
over lunch, I said there was an Italian
poet, Jacopone da Todi,
who lived in the Middle Ages, one day a building
collapsed, his wife was among those killed,
and when they undressed her to prepare
the body for burial he discovered
how all the years he had known her
she had been wearing a hairshirt.
There was something I wanted to add
in order to make the connection clear,
but I couldn't find words for it,

or I was afraid my feelings
might get the best of me. You know how
it is when you're speaking and you
begin to feel something enter
your voice, your voice
is always the first clue. To get this
quaver or catch out of my voice
as quickly as possible, I asked her
if irony was the word to describe
this situation, though I knew it wasn't,
I just wanted to put miles between
me and what I had said. But I'll tell you
something that is ironic. My mother's German
is superb, I've heard many people compliment
her on it, including Germans. Once when
we were in Amsterdam, she was buying
something from a street vendor.
She was addressing the man in German
since she knows no Dutch, but German
it became clear held very bad memories
for this man, he responded as if
she had been an enemy, not only German
but Nazi, an image probably reinforced
by her hair which was blond, though
she did not have her mother's blue eyes.
Back at the hotel she explained to me
what had been going on and how
strange it made her feel
because she's a Jew. My mother said
that would be the last time
she would speak German in Holland.
I have often wondered what my mother felt
when she taught me German songs, something she

did when we drove together on long trips.
I can remember her teaching me
"Heidenröslein" in the dark
as we drove over wooden bridges in the Carolinas.
She made me go over and over the pronunciation
until finally I knew the poem by heart
and eventually I sang it accompanying myself
on the piano. She had bought me
a book of Schubert's lieder. I played
the "Erlkönig," too, but "Heidenröslein"
was my favorite song. The story
is very simple, a boy picks
a rose because it is beautiful, he holds
it to his mouth because it is soft
and fragrant. But the rose
has promised to prick the boy
with her tough thorns
if he plucks her, and she does
prick him. Maybe
because Goethe's language is so plain
or maybe because my mother made me
practice the pronunciation so often
I still know the poem by heart.
I could even sing it for you, even now.

The Erl-King

Always at this hour and from far away,
who is it that practices the same time each day?

Always that obsessive patter of rain
striking at leaves, the same

unabating chatter. *Wer reitet so spät*
durch Nacht und Wind? Es ist

der Vater mit seinem Kind. And there came
Death riding faster, after. Always the same

mistakes, the errors driven
into fingers groping to find them.

But Death in his dark cloak riding
like wind through trees striding?

This is the month I was born. Late
afternoon is when it begins. How I hate

this hour of tepid aspics served
through plaster. It depresses. Never

from the beginning. Never
the closing notes. Interminable fever

of the middle, percussive failure of nerve.
With each new piece the teacher always gave

a little something I thought sent down
from a master, hands passing like a crown

to other hands the curve of disaster.
The teacher always creased a corner

of the page. Just so. I crossed
my thumb under, the muscles hoarse

from crying. The sound was a vine,
knotty, fibrous, in which fingers caught to climb.

But the sound disdains
the hand that reaches, pants, pains.

And so it goes. Proletariat flesh sweating to make
a world it can never enter. Take

a good look out the window. No one
seeks this building. No one departs. The phone

does not ring at this hour. Only hands
play over their errors, like sand

counting out the seconds. Turn the glass.
Mistakes spill in the other direction. As

for the pianist, the music turns on
like an electric timer. The pianist has gone

to Paris or to Rome. The dreadful playing comes on
with night. Could be, no one lives on

this street but me. Always at this hour,
always from far away comes the terror:

a pulse to beat alive what will not happen,
the repetitions of nothing moving, not even.

Feeding the Ducks at the Howard Johnson Motel

I wouldn't say I was dying for it.
But he was already undressed, trousers, socks, shirt
in a heap on the floor. Now it's four in the morning and he
wants to feed the ducks. I tell him the ducks are sleeping.
The ducks are awake, though, floating
around and around on the pond
like baby icebergs. It's a wonder they don't freeze,
it's a wonder there aren't videos
in every room with ducks clouding the screens.

When I was six, my parents took me
to the Jungle Queen, family dining, with portholes
over every table. Fish swam past my nose,
dull-whiskered carp, shadowy
as X-rays. I tried to squeeze crumbs
through the glass, but now I think those fish fed
on one another. He saved bread
from dinner, and throws a piece to the biggest
duck, paddling in circles. Even the taste

of our bodies comes from so far away,
from bodies and bodies where we have washed
ourselves clean and hard as stones.
If a duck shuddered into him, it would
shatter. If my tongue blew away, I might know
what to tell him. Instead, I say, Why does the orange
bedspread look hideous when duck feet, the same
color, are beautiful? He throws again
and again, the bread sinking right

in front of their beaks.
I have been hungry so long I could
lift an empty glass to my mouth and savor the air
for hours. Each time I throw bread
I feel like a child, my arm reaching out across
the pond, pitching as hard
as it can the fat balls of dough. Only
now I am aware of their dumbness,
their duck stupidity, how

they do not even see the bread, which glows
as it falls, every crust and crumb
shining under lights of the motel. Suddenly I
think of his teeth, hard
behind his lips; how, if a duck
bit me now, my hand
would open its heart, the rich
smell of something baking rising
from my flesh.

Night Music

Afterward, it sent me back to that passage in Chaucer
about the birds *that slepen al the nyght*
with open ye, and pretty soon that made me think
of another passage, in Coleridge, about
nightingales *perched giddily on blossomy twigs,*
their eyes both bright and full.
It wasn't long, though, before I thought of
a story by Chekhov I had read years ago
when I was in school, about a shy awkward man
at a party who takes a wrong turn and entering
a darkened room receives a kiss from a woman
who mistakes him for someone else, and later, when he
and the other officers are walking to their barracks
talking loudly and laughing, they hear
a nightingale singing in a bush
and gather round and touch
the bush, but the nightingale goes on singing.
That passage—I had to find the book under stacks
of others, following the underlinings to
the right place, but I don't mean
in my study where my books are,
I was far away in a motel, and then I had to go back
to the Chaucer again because I love to say
open ye, there is no sound in English today
like the ǭ in *open* and from there I had to do
giddily and *blossomy* again because *giddily*
would not be so giddy without the *y*
in blossomy and blossomy would not blossom, not
be so full of blossoms without the giddily. I had
to keep going back and forth, and probably
Chaucer and Coleridge and Chekhov
went walking at night in the woods, or
not in the woods, on country lanes.

Last night they awakened me
with their listening: and I thought this
must be a dream, so I lay there and let it happen
around me the way the men who shook the bush
must have dipped their hands in the wetness
of leaves and felt the music
close to their faces coming and going
like the breath of someone sleeping.
Something happened last night, already
I am losing it, and though it
wasn't a dream I should have held
a flashlight to the notebook I keep
by my bed and taken the trouble,
but the truth is, I hadn't the heart to move,
afraid if I stirred, the birds would stop
calling each to each
in the garden where the hibiscus and date
palms are, the calls muted, but clear,
the way you signal to someone in a darkened room
where others are sleeping, and then close by comes
the response, like a match struck.
It was the mockingbirds, the calls spaced far
apart at first, then contracting
in faster and faster threes. They sounded almost
human, birds imitating people playing games
in a garden, though no human
was down there, I looked, stepping out on the terrace.
And I can understand why the troubadors
imitated their calls
in motets and sestinas, and it's no wonder
so many of the troubadors were jugglers
for who wouldn't want to keep them airborne
as long as possible, whole flocks

resounding, a *summa,* a *speculum naturale.*
When I lived in Chicago
I practiced saying *pajama*
the way they say it there, the *a* more
drawn out and flatter than the *a*
in *jam, pi'jamma,* and when I was a child I had a friend
who said *cuffee,* and the place she came from
must have taken its time
standing on one leg in the kitchens
of its marshes and swamps. There were
sounds she could make, though
I never learned how, even after she let me
touch her throat and feel it there, quivering
a vibration more cicada
than bird. But the birds that night
were saying no more than they
had to, keeping it down, when possible, to one
note, packed. I could feel what pulsed
and pushed under the skin of that
music, and I would love to learn how
to do that, taking it from a bird's
mouth directly, the way Middle Eastern men
will kiss you after they have had a sip
of an aperitif you've never tried
so you can lick each sweet drop from their tongues.

Self-Portrait with Two Faces

Listen to the ocean, always raising
and lowering itself. Listen with your eyes closed.
Open the car windows, let the hot moist
air drift in and the murmuring. I used to go
for walks on a deserted beach,
a place where drops were made
routinely, though people were afraid
to touch the stuff when it washed up. Sometimes
it was morning. Sometimes I brought home
a shell. But because of the stars
I began taking walks at night.
There were so many stars. I lay on the cold
sand and looked up. At first I had romantic
thoughts. There is no need
to describe these. Everyone has them.
Then came strange, terrifying thoughts, so
peculiarly my own, I couldn't possibly
say what they were. Once I heard
the drone of a small plane
that must have been lost, circling, flying
upside down, mistaking the stars
in the hard black sea for the stars I stared up at.

If the way I said that made it sound
pretty, I'm sorry. Whenever I've tried to tell
anyone about those nights, the acoustics
go bad. We could be talking in Grand Central Station
or the Museum of Natural History. Echoes
bounce from marble wall to marble
floor, eddy in the hollows
and concavities where the voice, no longer
human, resounds like a famous peroration.
What? says my friend. *What?* But if I yell

the anonymity of light before the descent
the language feels wrong for the place
we're in, and by then the waitress
has brought our drinks and tacos and we've
settled into the subject of men
we once knew and forgot we remembered.

Nothing, I suppose, is ever forgotten, not
really, it goes on floating
like dust in swirls of light, and all through
the funny stories we told, I caught
glimpses I thought the better of. *Come on,*
says my friend, *you're holding back.*
Which was true, but they aren't stories,
more like moments—no, not even that.
Currents swing against one another,
impeding each other's progress through
a channel, my thinking dragged under, drowning
in its desire to be everywhere
at once, the rhythms overlapping in
the improvised sections, like a crowd
stampeding out of a burning
nightclub, pushed up against the other
crowd struggling to get in. But
by this time the story
is retracting itself, suddenly shy,
as if a stranger had joined
our table. *What? What? What?*
It's no use. The place is so noisy
we could be listening to a radio
in the tri-state area, with a joke
about the sex life of Santa Claus
breaking in from the next table.

He doesn't have any children
because he's gotta come down the chimney
seems to be the punch line
because everyone is laughing and the warmed-up
buzz is starting to work its hangover
sucking me back to the wordless
where what fills the ears
is water over and over sloshed.
Unanchored, each feeling
shoots up its flame, blossoming
into a thousand shapes and colors, a fireworks
of sensations, quick dream-burst
as if I had drifted off in the middle of
speaking, the echoes and sonic
booms demanding all my attention.

There must be whole lives
of feelings alien to language. Like microbes
that can live only thirty seconds
away from the body, they haven't a chance.
Or, if they make it, it's as a murmur.
Put your ear to a life, any life, and
there it is, the tell-tale tremolo, slur
and slap of the unexpressed, steady
rise and fall of something almost
abstract—the tie-dyed silks a life
slips on and off, the brailles when no one
spoke and only the rain started up
with its sound of someone peeing
in a vacant lot.
                                        That field is as close
as I ever come to what happened

between him and me, where I hesitate
on the outskirts, as if we two
were still on fire, miles of inner city
cordoned off, the listener barricaded
to a safe distance. If I could crush
that night like mint between my fingers
the aroma of sky over MacDonald's
might be the story, its sudden
crescendos of orange, its twist of greens.
It's a funny story, though
I can tell it crying, too,
even if it's tricky as rolling a wheel
down a hill, the voice holding on
with its one finger crooked. Language
makes me a stranger
to my own life, forcing me to speak
from both sides of my mouth,
a comic version for my friend,
a serious version for the one who
has joined us, sullen in his long blond hair
and blue shirt. Call me two-faced,

a Janus. Enamel my back
with snow, my face with May flowers.
Call me up, down, below, and
seat me, a dunce in a doorway. I'm a word
that splits on the tongue. Say *cleave*
and, Baby, I'll cleave
to you the way I cleaved him
in two and two and two, and clung
to every chopped up piece.

Only I don't want to tell it, I want
to watch, a private showing
on a private jet. Say, have you
ever flown into a great city
at sunset and floated among the broken
ice palaces of thirty thousand feet, the sun
blood-red, the air a ruin
of snow? Have you bathed in
that dazzle, in bubbles of light, a wisp
among wisps (the movie you half
watch between sips
of something that fills you
with its eloquence merely a pretext
for drifting) before you plunge,
seconds later, to find it's night
on the lower levels, the expressways, the office
buildings lit up against the dark?
It's that moment when the lights
surge on, but all the brightness
makes me want to do is sleep—
or rock back and forth in a loneliness
so immense I feel dizzy. Stars
are falling through it, nebulae
barren of life, pulsars, crowns, supernovas,
long strings humming, there's Pluto frosted
with methane, there's another planet—
hypothetical, still on the drawing board—
there are forms so exquisite no one could
inhabit them, coastlines with sand
that bends its flags in the wind
tracing a pattern which is neither
sand nor wind, the leaves
the stems still growing round

on themselves—hot young stars frothing
into intergalactic space, the lights
mirrored in puddles in glass walls,
the bridges speeding past.
Starstuff. Whatever I tried to say
about it over spiced chicken wings
at the revolving bar where I met with reps
from the other company kept sliding
into cliché. *Do you realize*
when it's dark down here, it's light
up there? But as soon as I said it
the looks on their faces
told me this was something kids
shove into your hands at airports, cheap
rose smelling of incense.
I threw it away.

Three

Women in Profile: Bas-Relief, Left Section Missing

Whatever it was they were celebrating
broke away, sheered off like ice

from a cliff. So they stand: three women
raising their glasses, toasting the air.

They might be sisters, they look so much alike,
or best friends, still inseparable,

hair sleeked back, their fluted skirts
grazing the stone that holds them in

perpetual festivity. They drink
to honor what is missing. Or they drink

to call it toward them, its music
still so far away no one has heard yet

its horns and timbrels. Or perhaps it's they
who have broken off, suddenly freed

like guests departed, their pockets stuffed
with cake wrapped carefully in paper

lace, turning one last time to toast
the musicians who have started up again, the pianist

playing the small bracelet of light someone
dropped in a corner, its endless variations.

Mosaic, Probably Narcissus

1

But something must have been happening before the
conversation—
a place for it, with a bronze commemorative statue, the
soldiers'
expressions pointing north and south and west.

Pigeons squatted on the bronze heads, the verdant rifles.

The statue did not set a mood for anyone

2

Unless absence of mood is also a mood: the park retreating at
dusk,
the tour of the condemned building where the floor gave way.
Now we look through what is no longer there to something
else. Perhaps if we are patient

a mood will come our way

3

Like a bus running late, but still welcome, the fumes and noise
signaling
presence, though not that presence in spring hardest to
breathe,
its color pollinated, viscous, vertiginous, a fountain
where doves syringe their wings.

4

What held that together was amniotic, an albumen, thickness
spilling from the cracked basin, as between fingers,
sperm seeping back or escaping. One dove grips
the stone rim with its powerful, hooked toes. Once I might
have said

about to pour itself in (the spoon dripping maple, molasses,
taffy, sap; the afternoons took that long then). Once
I might have said date palm, the rapid ablutions
of light in the pool and poured myself

into the swimming and those swimming, but especially into
the swimming which entered the water
browner and swifter than the swimmers, ahead and between, a
minnow
darting, tonguing, the compass needle undecided

(the larger, ponderous shadows of clouds piling up
at the bottom, along with the softer, more malleable)

5

But now I reject that

the way one changes one's mind about dessert
the can of free-stone peaches left unopened on the kitchen
counter
the pie of tropical fruits untouched, its finish

without fingerprint, its slices of kiwi untoppled, the sugarplum
pediment shellacked, chocolate buttresses unbroken, marbled
creams, cinnamon whispers, lusciousness stuck

to lusciousness, sweetness sweated out of sweetness,
the mother-of-pearl inlays, the opal glazes,
the patina iced, nail lacquer precious

but I have changed my mind

6

Or it's rejected the way a person elbows aside
a conversation suddenly boring, a person fidgeting at a bus
  stop
before walking off, the companion left behind, or a decade
abandoned, a certain style, a way of thinking

unbearable as the winter coats packed in mothballs
once it's summer. A person goes on seeing
the moment when it was suddenly boring

a moment no thicker than an eyelash or a watch hand
so tiny it can only be pinched with tweezers

placed carefully on the slide

a moment floating in serum its irresistible whirlpool of
  suggestions,
yet even under the microscope, it's not clear

who walked off, who was left behind, perhaps the moment
simply reached its destination and one of them
was no longer there, though a bench

was there, a man holding balloons was there and when
  someone
stepped down from the bus, there was a sense
of arrival, leaves swirling up, a roar
as the bus pulled away

7

However, and furthermore: the moment of rupture is not
  delicate.
It's as if a building had begun to separate, one part
of the century from the other, as if two streets—one cheek

then the other—a chasm opening between. Later, plywood
on the floor, placed carefully as if by a museum
curator, as we step over and around

the mosaic of doves and the shadow a bronze boy
casts upon the pool like bread
thrown—the shadow, a bronze and gold darkness

entering the water, rippling a breeze through it

8

What are the birds that come to drink there?

And are the waters healthful, but bad tasting, those bitter
salts dredged up at spas, the communal dipper plunged,
the head thrown back, each drinker Teresa
in ecstasy, the faces made—

or as Nietzsche understood, there are no beautiful surfaces
without dreadful depths.

So, all right, what kind of water lives in the imagination only?

9

The mood (just realized) I want for tonight is air-
conditioned, artificial, the subdued lighting
of suburban malls. I have let the girl with chartreuse
eye shadow, with topaz nails paint a new face
over the face I painted earlier

I am attracted to bad taste

I am attracted to exquisite taste

I'm in the mood for Chinese food, a large aquarium separating
the smoking from the no-smoking section

I'm in the mood for something fizzy and pink
I'm goose pimply for a drink
no longer in fashion, a Manhattan, the maraschino cherry

10

Once it was possible to walk through porticoes, the arches
at dusk, the enormous statuary balancing
stone wings. On the terrace dinner was served

in sonata form, there were recapitulations by candlelight
and codas, the hot washcloth tinged with lemon
while the boy, what we see of him, goes on

kneeling beside the pool, but now

it's the last moment as when one suddenly discovers
it's necessary to make a toast
and say something about the future, or more humbly, speak
of what we shall watch on TV tonight.

But as in those dreams where the mouth won't open
to scream, the boy does not move and the water does not
  move:

like a moth attracted to a mirror, floating the iced
finish of its wings, like a moth attracted
to flame, flutter given for flutter

though the flame keeps it up for longer, seemingly
inexhaustible, unquenchable—

the moment was like that, a foam in which we momentarily
vanished from language, the intensity of our gaze
burning up everything we might have said.

When we remembered the future
we sucked it dry,

it stopped moving, and we had to start it up again.

Aviary

When within the impenetrable
green this morning is (thicket, wicker
basket), the better to hear

shade in shadow, twigs and stabs
of light, I shut my eyes: the mockingbird
sings in threes, like Dante,

ninety-eight rhymes in
seventeen cantos; rocks throne
to throne, imbibing; wrings

out each note, scrubbing on
the old washboard, lets
the semitones soak

in the stillness. Once, twice,
can't get enough of. This way, the world
is not forgotten so fast

entirely. If you like I'll say
that again. Within
the impenetrable (whether or

not we're here to hear) goes on
scraps of song, trill, rapid drill
into tree, buzz and stub

of blue-dazzle flies chirred
on the wing, whatever scrape or jar
falsettoed, the bass twanging

protest down the throat. Gulped
once, recalled three times—
to mimic, the purest elegy. Morning's

gossip, radio left droning by
the pool, static worthy of remembrance,
repeated thirstily, can't get

enough of, so plays back
the playback, the button pressed to come
come again, keep coming, threaded

through the beak, *els letz*
becs
dels auzels ramencs. This one

bird grows the forest
thick and lush—it would take a machete
to cut the music: this bird sings

the branch it sings from, song
prehensile, probing the dark
irretrievable, leaf thrust

from beak, tongue blossoming: or
falls down rain, then
rises, the evaporate sucked

back: floats cage to
green cage spires and sprays, no
note so sour it cannot sweeten

my whistle squeezed, lemon
that puckers out the flavor. Prisoner
of the hedge and master, what calls

and what responds, antiphonal
continuo, squawk
box and intercom, repeat me repeating

blue jay, wing-whir and leaf
stir, the cardinal's kiss-the-back-
of-the-hand smack.

If singing came first, the voice
wavering above and below
what it means to grasp. If singing

came first, the string around
which clusters sense
and nonsense, rock candy

melting the mouth. To recall
one bird resounds
the amphitheater, the world

knotted to its single breath.
All it takes is one
note the lure thrown out to catch, one

to ambush the flock with
wow-wows, flutters, squeals, woomps
and a sixty-cycle hum. One

bird dropped down the abyss
splashes back, pumps
and primes the day with full fidelity

crossover network. Even the aromas
and the hush between boom
amplified: from Melos and Périgord, from

Siracusa, the ancient birdies prick-
eared, auricular, as Pound
hurls clumps of Greek

in the outdoor theater
where Chorus chanted warnings, left to
right, right to left, a wave advancing

retreating across the stage, lip
curled, Yeats chiming in
with "English poesy": its murmuring

bellowed (the first bird awake knows
its job is to crank the world
over and blow cold engines

to fury) until what growls up
is neither poetry nor Greek, a rumble
of foundations settling and resettling, as

if a rusty stylus had begun to turn
on the silence, that slur
when the deaf wind up to speak, the ear's

pegs not tight enough, voice
spilling its contours, rising
from the throat its yeasts.

The False Etymologies of Isidore of Seville

From, that's what he said, *from.* This one
from that, *eyrie* from *air,* so *ear* from *airy,* the ear
a nest that hears in air its own name.

Only those weren't the words he used.

I'm translating, his Latin swung like a censer, quorum of
birds over my head, their names out of reach
in the fragrant shadows, his chanting
what murmurs and luffs, clef on clef, major from
minor, augmented from diminished.

The way we pigged Latin I'm making this up, the way
we cupped the listener's ear, mushing
and watering the sounds, dotting and double
dotting the buzz and babble

sacheting our partners with a breeze of gossip.

Of Isidore little is known. When I see him
he's swallowing the pages of a book,
he's chewing the vellum, the illuminated letters
he's taking it from the hands of an angel
like a bird, soon he'll be a bird and fly away.

See, the interlaced letters of the alphabet
are tearing, word breaking from word, smudges of sound
on his fingers where he blotted the ink.

But no, I'm improvising. He stands untouched
in the florid zone where words
foam on the breath of saints, a world

sanctified, as when we rubbed our feet
on carpet and plucked sparks from our arms.

Twenty books of etymologies. The scriptorium
is cool in the morning, the marble
floors like a pool in which sandaled feet swim.

When he comes on the words, it's always afterward.
He touches to his tongue the golden powders
from which a fantastic initial F
for Fall, with mazy flourishes of plated leaves.

Why couldn't he have been there when it
all hung on the rim of the unsayable like droplets
of rain, a humidity he had only to wipe from his brow?

He wants to follow the initial S for Salvation,
pursue the long curve of the swan's
song back up the winding
throat and dab the first fruit with his own saliva.

He'll do it on hands and knees, the pilgrimage
of each word to its source, first sound
from which the others
bubbled up, original gurgling innocent of sense.

But I haven't his patience. I haven't got
all eternity. I skip to the parts I love best, the vowels
steeped like peaches in brandy, the hard sweet
suck of the pit, the wasp building up its
galls, nipple-tipped, velvety,
in spring a riot of reds and greens.

The language of pleasure is makeshift, leaves and branches
hastily thrown. Of mud and dribble.
Of huff and puff and higgledy-piggledy.
Of rampage, ruckus. Of blow your house down.

Fragment of a Woman from Kos

At first all you see are the folds
of drapery, high grass close together, swaying
beads you parted as a child, field behind
the house, then river. Sky.
You were told finches lived there, red-
winged, tipsy, upside down their hold
on the reeds, even so
they sang, trilling over and over
your outstretched hands song
poured like seeds from a basket or from
a bowl, water.
There was a woman,
young, beautiful—you used to hug her
from behind, closing your hands
over the cry of surprise
she gave out
like perfume. Now here
she is, rising
from the dead
landscape of memory, just this
fragment of her, still
kneeling.

Diluvial

Uprooted. Still glistening. Scratchy tough stalks with amber
berries.
With crabs, the orange claws opening and closing. With purple
Balloons and blue balloons advancing and retreating.
With glistening. With jaws still eating. With gateways and holes.
With funnels surprisingly cold.
With terraces of clouds impossible to walk across.
With a spiral stairway leading nowhere.
With spines, with bristles, with thorns still quivering.
With a large Sea Heart that has the ebony luster of a Baby
Grand.

With seven identical survivors glued to a ball of tar.
With seven from the dead man's chest. With Nickernut and
Starnut,
Box-Fruit and Yellow Flamboyant and a dove flown
From the Ark. With red ants come out at dusk, with
Something pierced by nails. With three warblers
That did not make it from the Bermudas, that
Lacked breath for the long flight, beaks still open.
With a green sequined fish no bigger than a thumbnail. It's
stiff.
With bird tracks crossing and recrossing, tern and piper and
one

Foot dragging. With rune and ogham and wedge, with futhark.
With a broken shell like an amphitheater.
With no regard for inventory, with the sibyl's leaves
Scattered, the messages polished but illegible.
With a black pearl from Cuba, with black suds, with a Black
  Mangrove
Already split and spitting roots. With thrust and heave and the
  suck back
Of each current named and spiraling wreckage
From Tobago and Trinidad, Dualo and Mozambique, Viti Levu,
  Fiji,
Wotho Atoll, Canton, Wahu Hawaii, Cocos-Keeling, Grand
  Cayman, the Cape of Good Hope.

With no regard for merchandise, with the salt
Spilled over and over for luck, for good measure, for the
  buoyant
Wood knocked on. With no understanding of containment,
Slopping in and out of the Agulhas Current, the Equatorial, the
  Kuroshino,
The Sirens far off course when Columbus sights them bobbing
In the Caribbean, their song unanchored, drifting
To leeward—Parthenope, Ligeia, Leucosia—like seaweed
  floating
Upward, the woman faces sunburned, freckled, "not
So beautiful as the painters made them,"

Their music pulling in different directions, the sailors
Transported, the tsunami raging far up the beach, the voices
Inundated, sucked down, note entangling
Note, the words no longer
In command, poured like water through a sieve, through the
   Gulf
Stream, with Mary's Bean through the five rivers of Hell, frigid
   Styx,
Mournful Cocytus, Acheron black and Phlegethon
Burning, Lethe remembering and forgetting
The cargo misplaced, the names of comrades lost, Ulysses still

Tied to the mast, "rolling from west to east
like a mountain" amid the multicolored silk awnings, amid
   palm
branches and gunnels, amid jib booms and chain plate, the
   landing craft
blown up, the jeep carriers missing, the sirens still wailing
on the guard ship, the deck in flames, the men jumping
overboard without pores and beakless, with surfaces bony or
fibrous—"Nor will I forget the drip and spackle
of zincs, the rough stuccoes of congealed metals"—
With seam and suture, with scars stellate and black knobbed,

with color dark brown to ochre to sepia gray, with the salt
spilled
over and over, the rich drift cracked and tumbled, unevenly
polished and sanded. "Nor will I forget the gold skin
skimmed from boiling lead, the fused mangle
of explosion, the run-off still running." "What happens if you
scrape
flame, if you cauterize fire?—that's what I'd like to know." Nor
will I forget the wings of Icarus, their wax still melting,
the failed flight commemorated, its ashes scattered
with the ashes of holocaust. Tied to the mast. Still listening.

From a Book of Prophets

1 The Return of Jonah by Way of Swanawic as Recorded by a West Saxon Scribe, 871 A.D.

Blown through the knothole, the tophole, the hole in its head
with the fat of whale on my hands and knees
with whale blubber sticking to me

Out of the gut maze, lifted up, drawn forth
I speak now through the jaw of the whale, through bone,
baleen, teeth not my teeth where the whale
breath wheezes, words whistle and sing—

Not my voice, whale voice, not my dream
I speak through *narwhal, squalus, cetus, hvalr*

Shut in, my flesh against whale flesh
head crammed into black vessels of whale blood
(yet I know nothing of whale)
under the heart smear, the brain wick, the tallow
mouth thick with dark
skidding and slippery the memory-child

Hvalr what the Norsemen said
Hwael what the kinsmen of Alfred threw all their might
sharpened like ivory, like the point of a star
into—the side, the flukes, the rolling belly
eye deeper than any hole
as they heaved out the bones blazoned
with the dark lineage of whale

And the women, faces anointed with the suint of sheep
chewing on their fatty lamps to hasten birth

Othere saw sixty in one day
But how can I number the dark the sheer weight
of the void defying measure
I who swam in whale blood, bedded in the divine clots
where the darkness rises and sets
knowing nothing of whale

Losing the word for water, I swam
Losing the word for breath, I sang
Losing the word for deep, I fell headfirst beating

2 The Furnace. A Bite, 1989

Three Hot Pokers, when they let us out we'd baked
blue and hard, that unforgettable paste
recovered from Persian tombs, but unbreakable.
Little guys, we did our soft shoe for
the politicians. Then God freed us to our
ordinary lives. Men of inflammable
faith, we walked right into another furnace.
Sure, we were hot stuff, our miraculous
survival stoked and heated by the media.
Well, we've told our story so often, tedium
is all we feel. Our advice to you
(if it happens to you)—Better to burn.
Take it from us, Shadrach, Meshach, Abednego.
Three little guys who did the soft shoe.

3 Boca Raton, 1990

Say the night was a cliff, a huge expectancy
the car climbed at right angles to a sky
floating its jets and fountains, its flimsy
chiffons of spray. I'm a sucker for beauty.
Besides, the seekers after comfort had gone
to the bar for daiquiris and drinks that foam.
Sometimes I dare myself to swim alone
where wind swells the imagination
black and something big as an ocean
takes a long drag, then heaves itself back.
When it happens, I don't want to come back.
Maybe I don't want to be believed.
Whatever it hisses into my ear, for me
only—unshared, undiluted, unsheathed.

Rapture

'Sing me something' is what the other keeps saying
night after night, regular as a pulse.

And when this one is alone, there's no problem.
He sings. He takes the lute-like
into his hands and plucks. Yes, he hears it.
What sounds like a sound. But when he opens his mouth,
it's different, it's the wrong sound.

Is it the acoustics inside
his head that make the difference? And who keeps
urging, making impossible demands
of him? 'Come on,'

the other one is saying like
a faucet dripping, like a branch beating the window.
The window in his head. He opens it.

'Come on, Caedmon, sing me hwaethwugu.' Yes,
that's how it sounds, like another
language, like gibberish, like
talking in his sleep. Remember the eensy-weensy

spider that climbed the water spout? That's how
he tries. His hands try. His lips.
It falls down. He tries. It falls down.
It's that regular. But when he makes it that regular
it's no good. It's not the same regularity.

I can't, he says, filling his mouth
with a big hole. Refusing, it begins for him.
Protesting, it swings itself up, it gets
going. It comes to him coming.

Or, it comes to her. What she lacks.
What hasn't happened in her
entire life, now it's coming, its absence
spread everywhere like a canyon in waves
of magenta and purple and gold.

The voice spreading before her. 'Forget
outside. Forget sky outside and clouds outside.'
This is what the voice spreads
before her, so she can look at what
it is saying. 'Forget heaps of dirt and yellowish brown
dust and gravel.' She passes through it,

a rift in her thinking where she lingers
so deeply and long
when she comes out of it, she can't remember
any more than a chasm spilling upward, clouds curling
an ocean of sound putting out stems
and branches of coral
which bend, break off, tempting

her body to match their motions. For a long time
she hears herself doing it, or I
hear her doing it,
in slow pendulations swept along, the bride
unbridling
in fetishistic foams and lace. The sound expanding
and stretching, blowing out
like bubble gum or Silly Putty.

The way a child flattens its nose and lips
against the glass of an aquarium
she pushes up against or I push up against

but when I go to say it, it sounds
different, hostile or angry with me, as if

I had seen
a gate opening in the dark
above my bed, a trellis on which light
grew and put out berries and thorns
of light and I

had blabbed instead of passing through.

Sky of Clouds

In that town in October
there was a ritual dressing up, a dance of sorts
that ended in a ballroom where a man laced
into a tight-fitting skirt and low-cut clingy blouse
asked me to dance. I am a woman talking
to you who exist like tinsel, a flash
and flicker at the periphery of my hearing.
On that floor were others
like me and others like him. He had managed
to extrude breasts that felt like
my mother's or my own, and we laughed about
that and the shade of his lipstick
was so close to mine, if we had kissed,
but someone cut in and stole him
from me. If this is shocking, let's say
I wanted to get your attention fast
like a neon sign or the lush trees
where I live. In spring they hang out
their ovaries in red and yellow
clusters, and they don't let you
get away any more than the women who walk
along the highway with only their poverty
and their dark hair let you
miss what they want from you. But
my subject is not what it seems. I want
to explain how it is for me
all the time now whether I'm dancing
or propped on pillows watching
the scarlet streaks of heaven, the orange
fronds of the weather. The birds
kill me with their singing, the saddest songs
are sung at sunset, and I stir the ice
in my drink and let it go, remember

and let it go, which is what the wind
does with everything I love. Sometimes,
I can't help it, I have to
get in the car and play toccatas and fugues.
I have to look at the clouds,
fat ladies on their couches, the green
and gold tassels of a sumptuous life
that keeps changing its liqueurs and girdles,
the slow slide of its trombones. Over the ocean
pelicans plummet, so heavy
with desire, it sinks them deep
as rivets, as pile drivers into
whatever catches their eye for the moment.
And after heavy rains, when the egrets
settle on the gardens, cramming
their beaks with the shrill
cries of the frogs, I think
I could do that too, I could be gorgeous and cruel.
But it's more magnanimous than that.
Right now clouds are what is going on, and after
the clouds come violet and blue. The deep
purples, the lavish tangerines
so extreme, you suspect this isn't happening,
this has been touched up. Flaming
effluvium, wells in the music
where sound bubbles, and you slide down
or through, brown rings within lime
rings, ferriferous bracelets.
Toward this hour a dark gray wading
bird comes to drink the water in the swimming pool,
a saliva color restores to the mouth. *Hello,*
strange bird, with a taste for chlorine.
Very slowly, as if arthritic, it dips

deep into its own transparency. I think
it drinks. I think it is not a mechanical
prank someone has left there. Its
throat muscles are moving.